D1242501

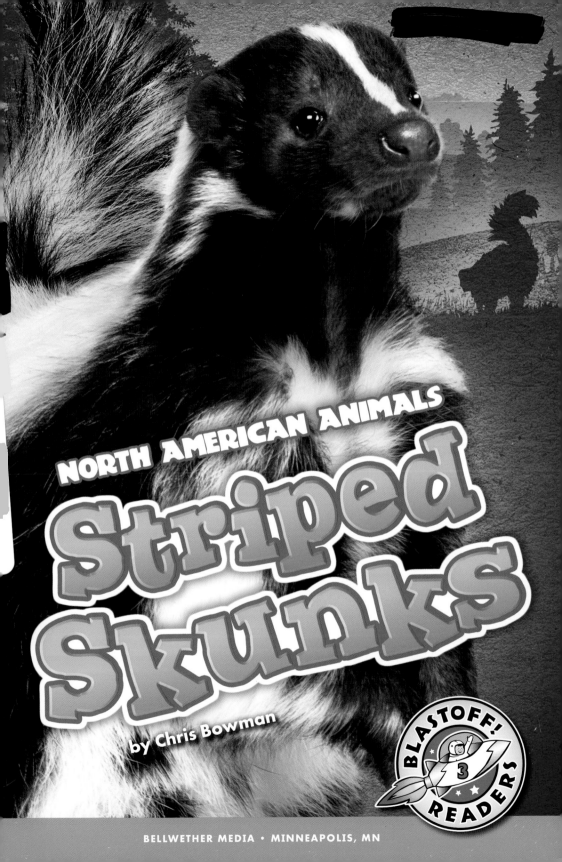

NORTH AMERICAN ANIMALS

Striped Skunks

by Chris Bowman

BELLWETHER MEDIA • MINNEAPOLIS, MN

BLASTOFF!
3
READERS

Note to Librarians, Teachers, and Parents:

Blastoff! Readers are carefully developed by literacy experts and combine standards-based content with developmentally appropriate text.

Level 1 provides the most support through repetition of high-frequency words, light text, predictable sentence patterns, and strong visual support.

Level 2 offers early readers a bit more challenge through varied simple sentences, increased text load, and less repetition of high-frequency words.

Level 3 advances early-fluent readers toward fluency through increased text and concept load, less reliance on visuals, longer sentences, and more literary language.

Level 4 builds reading stamina by providing more text per page, increased use of punctuation, greater variation in sentence patterns, and increasingly challenging vocabulary.

Level 5 encourages children to move from "learning to read" to "reading to learn" by providing even more text, varied writing styles, and less familiar topics.

Whichever book is right for your reader, Blastoff! Readers are the perfect books to build confidence and encourage a love of reading that will last a lifetime!

This edition first published in 2016 by Bellwether Media, Inc.

No part of this publication may be reproduced in whole or in part without written permission of the publisher. For information regarding permission, write to Bellwether Media, Inc., Attention: Permissions Department, 5357 Penn Avenue South, Minneapolis, MN 55419.

Library of Congress Cataloging-in-Publication Data

Bowman, Chris, 1990- author.
  Striped Skunks / by Chris Bowman.
    pages cm. – (Blastoff! readers. North American Animals)
  Summary: "Simple text and full-color photography introduce beginning readers to striped skunks. Developed by literacy experts for students in kindergarten through third grade"– Provided by publisher.
  Audience: Ages 5-8.
  Audience: K to grade 3.
  Includes bibliographical references and index.
  ISBN 978-1-62617-338-5 (hardcover : alk. paper)
  1. Striped skunk–Juvenile literature. 2. Skunks–Juvenile literature. I. Title. II. Series: Blastoff! readers. 3, North American animals.
  QL737.C248B69 2016
  599.76'8–dc23
                        2015028689

Printed in the United States of America, North Mankato, MN.

Table of Contents

Striped skunks are **mammals** found all over the United States. Some call southern Canada or northern Mexico home.

Extinct

Extinct in the Wild

Critically Endangered

Endangered

Vulnerable

Near Threatened

Least Concern

striped skunk range =

conservation status: least concern

Most striped skunks live near water in forests and grasslands. Others live in cities.

bushy tail   white stripes   triangular head

Striped skunks have black fur. Two white stripes begin at their heads and run down their bodies. Their tails are a mix of black and white.

The skunks have short legs. **Webbed feet** and long claws help them dig for food.

Striped skunks are about 18 to 32 inches (46 to 81 centimeters) long from nose to tail. They can weigh up to 14 pounds (6 kilograms).

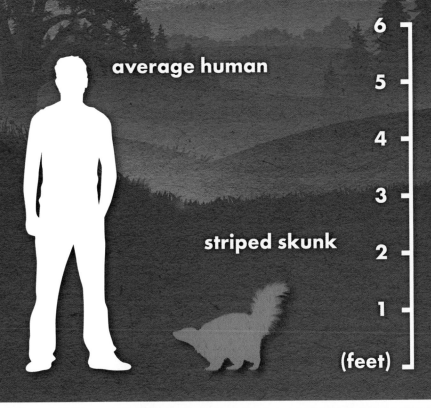

Size of a Striped Skunk

average human

striped skunk

6
5
4
3
2
1
(feet)

Males are often bigger than females.

The skunks are famous for their **defenses**. When scared, they stamp their feet and raise their tails.

They also spray their **scent** at **predators**. The mist smells bad and hurts eyes. The scent is hard to get off.

bald eagles

great horned owls

golden eagles

coyotes

bobcats

red foxes

A striped skunk's spray does not keep all predators away.

Birds such as owls and eagles often take their chances. Sometimes, other animals are hungry enough to attack.

Finding Food

Striped skunks are **nocturnal**.
These **omnivores** come out
at night to eat.

On the Menu

grubs

bees

black cherries

deer mice

red-legged
grasshoppers

spotted
sandpiper eggs

They use their claws to dig for
grubs. They also search for small
mammals, fruits, and bird eggs.

The skunks often sleep in **dens** underground. They look for empty **burrows** dug by other animals.

Sometimes striped skunks dig their own burrows. They may also rest in **hollow** logs or under buildings.

In cold areas, striped skunks
spend the winter underground.
Several skunks sometimes share
one den to keep warm.

They are less active during winter. They often do not eat until spring!

Females give birth to **kits** in the spring. The babies **nurse** for about six weeks. Then the young skunks learn to find food on their own. Time to leave mom!

Name for babies:	kits
Size of litter:	2 to 10 kits
Length of pregnancy:	about 2 months
Time spent with mom:	up to 1 year

Glossary

burrows—holes or tunnels that some animals dig for homes

defenses—ways of keeping an animal safe

dens—sheltered places; striped skunks rest in dens underground, in hollow logs, or under buildings.

grubs—very young beetles

hollow—empty through the middle

kits—baby skunks

mammals—warm-blooded animals that have backbones and feed their young milk

nocturnal—active at night

nurse—to drink mom's milk

omnivores—animals that eat both plants and animals

predators—animals that hunt other animals for food

scent—an odor or smell

webbed feet—feet with thin skin that connects the toes

To Learn More

AT THE LIBRARY

McGill, Jordan. *Skunks*. New York, N.Y.: AV2 by Weigl, 2012.

Miller, Connie Colwell. *The Stinkiest Animals.* Mankato, Minn.: Capstone Press, 2011.

Owen, Ruth. *Skunk Kits*. New York, N.Y.: Bearport Pub., 2011.

ON THE WEB

Learning more about striped skunks is as easy as 1, 2, 3.

1. Go to www.factsurfer.com.

2. Enter "striped skunks" into the search box.

3. Click the "Surf" button and you will see a list of related web sites.

With factsurfer.com, finding more information is just a click away.

Index

The images in this book are reproduced through the courtesy of: Eric Isselee, front cover, p. 6 (bottom); David Burke, p. 4; James Coleman, p. 6 (top left, center, right); blickwinkel/ Alamy, p. 7; age fotostock/ Alamy, p. 8; Big Pants Production, p. 10; Wild Images/ Kimball Stock, p. 11; FloridaStock, p. 12 (top left); mlorenz, p. 12 (top right); withGod, p. 12 (center left); Cynthia Kidwell, p. 12 (center right); Svetlana Foote, p. 12 (bottom left); Geoffrey Kuchera, p. 13; Alan G. Nelson/ Age Fotostock, p. 14; Melinda Fawver, p. 15 (top left); irin-k, p. 15 (top right); Olha Rohulya, p. 15 (center left); Close Encounters Photo, p. 15 (center right); Paul Reeves Photography, p. 15 (bottom left); Vishnevskiy Vasily, p. 15 (bottom right); James Hager/ Robert Harding World Imagery/ Corbis, pp. 16-17; birdphotos.com/ Wikipedia, p. 18; Mircea Costina, p. 19; Gordon & Cathy Illg/ Age Fotostock, p. 20; Juan Martinez/ Superstock, p. 21.